BRAIN-SWITCH

A Dramatically Effective Treatment

for Healing Traumatic Memories

by

Judi Craig, Ph.D. and Jonathan Rice, Ph.D.

First Printing August 2012

Printed in the United States of America
ISBN-978-0-9705648-4-9

Dedication to Andrea Rice, LCSW-ACP

We dedicate this book to the loving memory of Andrea—Jonathan's late wife who founded the Institute of NLP in Austin, TX (and later Co-Directed the Institute with Jonathan until her death in 2000). Andrea was Judi's first NLP trainer.

NOTE TO READER

This book is intended for psychotherapists and counselors. While the focus in teaching the BRAIN-SWITCH process in our first few chapters is for healing trauma from Post Traumatic Stress Disorder, we use the same process for all types of clinical problems including anxiety, anger, depression, low self-esteem, phobias, belief changes, abandonment, rejection, criticism and other common issues clients bring to psychotherapists. You will find many case studies in the PUTTING THE PROCESS TO WORK chapter that illustrate our work with other issues besides PTSD.

While the BRAIN-SWITCH process can be used as a self-help tool for everyday aggravations, it usually requires a psychotherapist for deeper work. Many clients who have engaged in the process a few times with a psychotherapist are then able to use it successfully as a self-help tool for minor aggravations.

INTRODUCTION

Jonathan is the brains behind BRAIN-SWITCH. As a clinical psychologist and Neurolinguistic Programming trainer, he has always been interested in the way the brain works. About 13 years ago, influenced by new research on brain plasticity, he began experimenting with a process based on brain functioning that would help his clients heal from traumatic experiences, past or present. And he wanted a process that wouldn't take months or years of psychotherapy to really make a difference in his clients' lives.

BRAIN-SWITCH was born! As he worked with the process over the next couple of years, he knew from the results he was getting with his clients that he had innovated a truly helpful tool for psychotherapists. But before letting the world know about the process, he wanted to make sure it was a *teachable* tool that other therapists could use with the same positive results.

He invited 15 colleagues to a training on BRAIN-SWITCH (Judi was one of them). The group met one weekend a month for three months. They learned the process, began using it with their own clients, and reported back to the group the results they were getting—as well as any problems they encountered. Since the training, those therapists—and the people they have taught the process—have found BRAIN-SWITCH to be a dramatically effective tool in their work with clients. And the process has wide application; it is effective not only with reconfiguring traumatic memories, but for many issues for which patients consult therapists.

It is not unusual for clients who have Post Traumatic Stress Disorder (PTSD)—whether from combat, sexual abuse, or other stressors—to heal a *specific* traumatic incident in one session.

To find out how, read on.

TABLE OF CONTENTS

- HOW BRAIN-SWITCH CAME ABOUT

- HOW MEMORIES CAN SCARE US

- REPRESENTATIONS 101

- THE PROCESS

- PUTTING THE PROCESS TO WORK

- WHAT IF YOU GET STUCK?

- FINAL THOUGHTS

Appendix A: Joseph LeDoux, Ph.D.

Appendix B: PTSD Questionnaire for Clients

Acknowledgments

References

About the Authors

HOW BRAIN-SWITCH CAME ABOUT

With the wars in Iraq and Afghanistan, there has been increased public awareness of Post Traumatic Stress Disorder (PTSD), present both in active duty military men and women as well as in veterans. Returning from combat or deployments in a war zone, many serving in our military have highly traumatic memories from witnessing the horrible things that happen in war.

Although psychiatrists and psychotherapists have been treating victims of PTSD for many years—from sexual assault, fires, robberies, car accidents, shootings, natural disasters and other traumas—the surge of people suffering from trauma related to our recent wars has given new impetus to finding innovative ways to treat the symptoms of PTSD. Whereas other victims of PTSD typically have symptoms from one traumatic *incident*, those returning from war have often had *repeated* and *chronic* exposure to traumas. These can include a specific event or a number of them, or the traumatic event may simply have occurred most of the time they were in a war zone (as in spending months in almost continual fire fights or mortar attacks, or being a medic taking care of the wounded during an entire deployment).

The psychotherapy approach currently thought most beneficial for PTSD is Cognitive Behavioral Therapy (CBT). Two types are commonly used: Cognitive Processing Therapy (CPT) and Prolonged Exposure Therapy (PET). In CPT (done individually or in groups), patients are asked to question distorted thinking patterns stemming from their war experiences that keep them in a state of sensory hyper-arousal where they perceive danger when none logically exists. They are asked to question their distorted thoughts about their guilt over things they witnessed or did during the war, realizing that tragic things occur in the heat of combat or when one's life is threatened. Patients are encouraged to look logically at their distorted thoughts and to change them.

In PET, patients are asked to talk about, write about, and visualize their traumatic memories with intense focus and clarity, often even using audiovisual media to fully immerse the patient in all aspects of the traumatic event(s). The idea is that by repeatedly re-living those upsetting experience(s) in their minds, the memories eventually will no longer elicit anxiety, guilt or other unwanted reactions.

While some people have benefited from these treatment approaches, many have not. Just talking about their traumatic memories, especially in the more intense PET method, many of our clients tell us that the process is too painful. For example, if they were having nightmares about their traumas two to three times a week, they may start having nightmares two to three times a night when they began PET. Patients have told us that their PTSD symptoms worsened to the point where they lost faith in the treatment and dropped out of therapy. Many veterans talk about having months or even years of psychotherapy with these approaches without their symptoms improving. And the most vivid of the symptoms—nightmares and flashbacks—often continue even when the person has managed to gain control over other symptoms such as irritability and anger. While patients can find value in just "letting it out" and telling a sympathetic, non-judgmental human being about the horrors they experienced, most have not even spoken about them to their spouses and families. The symptoms keep continuing.

Another treatment approach for PTSD is Eye Movement Desensitization and Reprocessing (EMDR). The patient is asked to think about a traumatic event while rapidly moving his/her eyes following the quick movement of a therapist's pencil or finger. The rapid eye movements involve bilateral stimulation of both brain hemispheres. The idea is that this process helps patients to remember their traumatic experiences without having to endure the emotional pain. (EMDR has some similarities to BRAIN-SHIFT, which also has to do with specific eye movement and bilateral stimulation of the brain hemispheres resulting in the ability to remember the trauma without the emotional pain or without "triggering" an unwanted emotional response). However, studies on the effectiveness of EMDR have had mixed reviews for PTSD, and the method requires many hours of training (as does PET). In contrast, BRAIN-SWITCH can be effectively taught to therapists in just a few hours and used in their offices the next day.

BRAIN-SWITCH was born out of current brain research on

neuroplasticity and the fields of Neurolinguistic Programming and EMDR. Additionally, Jonathan began to experiment with how a client's internal experience changed based on whether he was looking out of his left or right eye. With one eye, he had access to his emotions; with the other, he did not. For example, Jonathan would place an eye patch over a person's right or left eye, have him talk about an emotional experience, and find that—depending on which eye was covered—the person would speak emotionally when one eye was covered but talked logically and without emotion about the same experience when the other eye was covered. And which eye was which was different for different people. However, the majority of people are more emotional when their left eye is covered and they are viewing the trauma with the right eye. (Note: We have found that, for some currently unexplainable reason, covering one's own eye with hand or paper cannot be substituted for using an eye patch).

In a workshop demonstrating this phenomenon, Jonathan placed an eye patch on the left eye of a person who was known for being highly intellectual and for responding to events in a very rational manner. The person became confused about how to respond to questions about a personal issue, reported that he felt overwhelmed, and even began crying.

In another demonstration, Jonathan placed an eye patch on the left eyes of two close friends, asking them to discuss a topic. Their easy interaction and fondness for one another was obvious. When the eye patches were switched to their right eyes, they reported (and the workshop participants observed) that their previously natural and smooth manner of interacting became stilted and strained. Both reported being very uncomfortable until the eye patches were removed.

Work with the eye patch was instrumental in developing the BRAIN-SWITCH process. If a person can become more emotional or more logical/rational about an emotional event depending on which eye she is looking out of, could a person's recalling a memory by visualizing it with one eye versus the other change the degree to which she experiences strong emotion when thinking of that memory.

We know that our experiences—and the way we see/hear/feel them—are stored in a particular way in our brains. Change the way you see/hear/feel these experiences in your brain, and you can change their emotional impact. BRAIN-SWITCH is a relatively quick process that alters the way the brain stores emotional experiences so patients no longer have (or experience a great reduction in) the negative emotional reactions triggered by those experiences.

For example, let's imagine that you had been raped 10 years ago in a parking garage during a thunderstorm. Now, when you hear thunder, you get a knot in your stomach. And you can't even drive in a parking garage. After a BRAIN-SWITCH, you would remember that you had been raped and could talk about it if you wanted to. But you would no longer be "triggered" by a thunderstorm to get a knot in your stomach, and you would be able once again to drive in a parking garage.

HOW MEMORIES CAN SCARE US

We all record images, sounds, smells, tastes and touches in our brains. For example, think of the face of your child, the sound of your favorite music, the smell of chocolate chip cookies in the oven, the taste of a lemon, the feel of your first kiss. We also remember exciting experiences: riding a roller coaster, being splashed by cold ocean waves, or the sensation of someone rear-ending us in traffic. All of these sensations and experiences produce feelings of varying intensity.

Neurobiologists tell us that the more exciting the experience, the more parts of our brains may be involved in creating our memories. The organ in our brains that becomes involved when we are frightened is called the amygdala, producing a "flight or fight" response. If an experience threatens our lives (or is perceived to threaten our lives), the amygdala records the intensity of the event in all sensory channels - images, sights, sounds, smells, and feelings. A person may only remember the feelings and a few fleeting images or sounds of an experience - or may be able to access the entire memory - and the memory may be stored in his conscious or unconscious mind.

Patients who have experienced trauma, as in those with PTSD, can have those traumas re-activated via their sensory channels even when no danger is present. An image, sound, smell, taste or feeling can "trigger" memories that have been stored in their amygdalas. For example, a combat veteran can see a dead animal at the side of a road and be "triggered" to swerve sharply when no real danger is present, remembering the IED that was planted inside a dead animal when he was in Iraq. He may have to sit with his back against the wall so he can have a clear view of the door and all the occupants in a restaurant so as not to be surprised by an attacker barging through the door, his amygdala causing him to respond as if he was still at war.

So what is happening in the brain during a BRAIN-SWITCH process? The reality is that we really don't know—and probably won't until neuroscientists examine a patient's brain before and after a BRAIN-SWITCH or while the process is being carried out. But our speculation is that when a BRAIN-SWITCH has occurred, the amygdala will no longer be involved when the traumatic event is remembered.

REPRESENTATIONS 101

If someone asked you to tell them the number of rooms in your house, most likely you would have to first picture your house in your mind and quickly count the rooms. Now you might not be aware as you're counting that you are actually making a picture of your house in your mind's eye - you probably would think you're just "thinking" about your house and counting the rooms. If someone said to you, "Picture your house" or "Make a visual image of your house in your mind", you'd be more aware of the picture your brain is actually making. And that picture in your mind's eye is what we would describe as *representing* the way you think about your house.

Now when you have a memory of something—a person, a house, a room, an animal, a city, a conversation, an experience— when doing the BRAIN-SWITCH process, you would be asked to *represent* that memory in any way that occurs to you. And that *representation* would be very individualized. Two people thinking of the same person would *represent* that person very differently based on their perceptions and history with that individual. One might see the person with kind eyes, smiling face, and a loving demeanor; the other might see that same person with stern eyes, an angry look, and a disapproving demeanor. And each of us could imagine the same person as "loving" one time and "disapproving" the next depending on the particular memory of that person we were having at that particular moment. So there are innumerable ways that we can *represent* anything we are thinking about.

While most people can make visual *representations* of whatever they are thinking about, some of us must make auditory *representations*; we must talk to ourselves before we can make a mental picture. If asked to remember a situation, there is no obvious picture or visual image—just sounds and conversation from that situation and/or mental self-talk (what we say to ourselves) about that situation. Working with a person who doesn't make immediate mental pictures, we first ask the client to locate the feeling in her body when she thinks of the memory. Then we ask her to be aware of any sounds or self-talk that accompany the feeling—and *then* to create an image or picture. With BRAIN-SWITCH, we need to get the client to remember an image or picture that occurs with the sounds and/or with self-talk. So her auditory *representation* can then lead to a visual *representation*.

For a BRAIN-SWITCH to be successful, it is very important that we *represent* our memories in the most vivid way, including any tastes, smells, feelings, sounds and visual pictures that occurred. For example, if asked to *represent* a time when you were slapped by your father, you would be asked to include the sound of the slap, the smell of your father's cologne, perhaps the taste of the gum you were chewing at the time, and your feelings of fear and/or anger as he slapped you. In any particular memory, there may be no smells or tastes or sounds or feelings or pictures - but the *representation* must include any of the senses that were part of that particular memory to make that *representation* as vivid as a client's memory will allow.

To illustrate the *representation* process, let's take a look at some examples:

- Your boss just told you that you were going to be laid off due to a decline in company profits. Your visual *representation* of that moment might be a picture including you and your boss sitting in his office, the sound of his voice, your growing anxiety as you realized what he was saying to you, and the smell of the leftover lunch sitting on his credenza. If you are someone who has to talk to yourself before you can create the visual *representation*, you might be saying something to yourself like "I am in my boss's office and he is telling me I'm going to be laid off. I feel anxious. I smell his left-over lunch on the credenza."

- You are a soldier who is remembering a traumatic moment during combat. Your visual *representation* is a mental picture of the Humvee that was in front of you being blown up, the sounds of screaming, the heat from the fire, and the smell of burning flesh. If you have to talk to yourself, you would tell yourself what happened: "I'm watching a Humvee right in front of me blow up; the fire is hot. I hear screaming and I smell burning flesh." You have made an auditory *representation* that then can bring about the visual *representation*.

- You want to create a *representation* of your mother's being highly critical of you as you were growing up. You visualize a particular instance that took place in the kitchen where you lived, hear the tone of her voice, feel your irritation with her remark, and smell the bread that was baking in the oven. If you have to talk to yourself before you can create a visual *representation*, you might say something like "I'm in the kitchen and hear my mother criticizing me. I'm really irritated. I smell bread baking." This process then allows you to make the visual *representation*.

One can certainly create *representations* of the positive experiences in one's life as well as negative ones, such as when we re-live in our minds a wonderful memory that brings about positive emotions. But the above examples all illustrate negative experiences for the person involved because BRAIN-SWITCH is about taking the emotional trauma away from negative memories so they can be dealt with in a more logical, unemotional manner that no longer triggers upsetting feelings.

Now that you know what we mean by *representations*, you're ready to learn the BRAIN-SWITCH process!

THE PROCESS

To learn how to do the BRAIN-SWITCH process, we'll use an example that many men and women who have been in combat have experienced: Having mortars fired at or near them (a mortar is an indirect fire weapon that fires explosive projectiles known as mortar bombs at low velocities, short ranges, and high-arching ballistic trajectories). In these situations, soldiers can hear a mortar coming but cannot predict where it will land, increasing the feeling of helplessness not knowing where to go to avoid being hit.

For ease in writing about the process, we'll ask you to imagine that you are the soldier struggling with the memory of a mortar attack so we can use the language we would actually use in a therapy session. What we would say to you as a client will be printed in **bold.** Non-bolded text is a message to the reader.

Of course, we are assuming that you have sufficient rapport with the client, that you are sensitive to the client's pace, and that you modify our wording as necessary.

Step 1. Notice how you feel.

When you think about that mortar attack, what do you feel? Where in your body do you notice the feeling (tightness in chest, shaky feeling in upper body, lump in throat, knot in stomach, warmth or coldness, tingling, etc.). The feeling may be very strong or just barely noticeable.

While most people remembering a combat experience have no trouble getting in touch with their feelings, what if a client is not aware of any feelings in his body? We would ask the client to change his posture by sitting up with feet flat on the floor and not crossing his legs, ankles, feet, arms, hands or fingers. By assuming this posture, the client typically can identify the feelings he has when he thinks about the mortar attack.

We want you to be very aware of your feelings or physical sensations as you think about this experience so you'll be able to know after the BRAIN-SWITCH process if those feelings are still present (they won't be if the BRAIN-SWITCH has been successful).

Step 2. Represent the experience.

Imagine that mortar attack (or one that is representative of the many you may have experienced). You can probably make a picture in your mind's eye about this situation. While making the mental picture, imagine any sounds, smells, tastes or feelings you had during the event. As you are making a visual image of this in front of you, notice if your mental picture is on the left or the right side of your nose.

If the client is unable to make a picture, we would say the following: **I want you to get in touch with the feeling you have as you remember the mortar attack. What are you hearing and is it located on the right or left side of you? What are you saying to yourself? You might be hearing the sounds of the mortar attack(s), including not only the sound of the mortars but also the sounds other soldiers around you were making ("Get to the bunker", "It's coming from the hill", moaning from someone who was hit, etc.), other sounds from the environment (sirens, alarms, commands, etc.) and/or what it is that you said to yourself when you were having the experience ("Fuck", "This is it", "I'm never going to get out of here", etc.). Now make a picture of the attack based on those sounds you heard and what you were saying to yourself.**

When a client is imagining the attack, what if he is not sure whether he is seeing/hearing it on the left or right side of his body? What if he is imagining the picture or sound as coming from out in front of him, or behind him? We would tell him: **Deliberately move the mental picture/sound of your experience from the right to the left (or vice versa). Which side produces the stronger upsetting feeling inside you? One side will feel more emotional, the other much less so.**

Why worry about the right or left side? Because you want the client to locate which side *in his mind* holds his emotionally upsetting experiences (it will be the same side for any emotionally upsetting experience) in order to execute the BRAIN-SWITCH. We reassure clients that there is no "right" or "wrong" side—it's just the way his brain organizes his experiences.

Note that we're not talking about right or left hemispheres of the brain. We're talking about the location *out in front of the client* where his mind's eye sees the experience.

Step 3. Imagine an ugly container.

On the same side of your body where you see the mental picture, imagine some type of ugly container. It could be a black leaf bag, a dumpster, a garbage can, a bucket, a battered trunk, a biohazard container—any type of container. What you're going to do in the next step is to imagine putting all your upsetting experiences relating to the mortar attack(s) into this container.

We do ask the client to tell us what type of container he has chosen and to describe it (size, color, etc.) so that we can refer to it correctly.

Step 4. Get the history of the client's experience.

In this step, your purpose is to gather all the memories associated with the experience of mortar attacks and represent them fully—including any pictures, sounds, smells, tastes or feelings that were associated with the attack(s). As you recall each memory clearly, you're going to imagine placing that memory in your ugly container. Use your imagination freely.

If the client asks *how* to represent the memory, we suggest he make either a snapshot, a collage, a video or an audiotape. For example, in making a visual image of mortar attacks, he may find it easier to imagine a brief video (about three seconds long, not "real time") of the entire event, or just a snapshot that captures the memory. In making an audiotape or CD, he might hear the voices and sounds of the attack - including what he was saying to himself during the attack - and then dump the audiotape or CD into the container.

Now think of any other experiences you have had that are somehow related to the mortar attacks. For example, maybe after an attack occurred, you saw the bodies - or body parts - of soldiers around you who had been killed. Maybe you remember yourself later the same day sitting alone and crying about those deaths. It is even possible that the mortar attack(s) trigger some childhood memory. For example, perhaps your house was shot up in a drive-by shooting or you witnessed a friend who was playing around with a gun and accidentally shot someone or shot himself. The idea is that any images or sounds that remind you of the mortar attack(s) would belong in the container.

We would continue asking you, **"What other memories are triggered by this particular experience?"** We want our clients to take the time to think about this because stopping the process too soon may miss some very significant memories. So we keep asking, **"What else? What else is there in your unconscious mind that relates in some way to mortar attacks?"** until we feel comfortable that the client has sufficiently explored this question.

Then, just to be sure, the therapist makes this strong statement: **"So there is nothing else that your unconscious mind needs you to remember about this issue to be complete."** As a therapist, you will feel more confident that everything is in that container that belongs there when this statement brings up a solid, congruent "No" from the client.

What if the client reports numerous instances of mortar attacks? Sometimes is it easier for the client to make a mental collage of those similar experiences and then place the entire collage into the container. If a client asks if she should place the images of those experiences into the container one at a time or in a collage, we say something like **"Just do what feels right to you intuitively."**

The point is, it is not necessary for a person to get *every* representation of *every* mortar attack. Just the major aspects of those experiences need to be in the container.

Step 5. The "switch".

Now you are going to learn to mentally "switch" the ugly container from the side of your body where you've been imagining it to the opposite side. By doing so, you'll be moving the emotional memories in the container to a place in your brain where they can be remembered in a logical, less-emotional way. You will still remember these experiences, but they will no longer trigger the emotional reactions (terror, rage, grief, hurt, etc.) that you've been having from those experiences. In this specific example, you'll still remember the mortar attack(s), but no longer startle (or startle as badly) with loud noises, or have negative physical symptoms (sweating, shaking, nausea, etc.) when you remember the attack(s). *And if you have been having nightmares of those attacks, those nightmares should cease*

(assuming you have not had a significant aspect of a mortar attack memory that you didn't think of putting into the container).

But before you do the "switch", you need to ask yourself two very important questions: **"Is there any part of you that would not want you to eliminate your negative emotional reaction to memories of mortar attacks?"** Then double check by asking yourself, **"So all parts of you agree that nothing bad or negative will happen to you if you no longer get triggered into negative emotions when you think about the attack(s)?"** If the client doesn't feel comfortable—or there is even the slightest hesitation—as you ask him those questions, the client is not ready to proceed with the "switch". (We'll discuss what to do if you do become aware of discomfort or hesitation in the next chapter).

To execute the "switch", you're going to stare *straight out in front* of *you* (eyes closed or open, whichever is easier for you) and imagine moving the ugly container from the side where you've had it (right or left) to the *opposite* side—*but in a very specific way.* There are two critical things to remember in order to do it successfully.

- *You must not have any part of your body crossing another part*—no crossed arms, hands, fingers, feet, legs or ankles. While sitting, place both feet flat on the floor and make sure your hands/arms are not crossed. Do not do this while lying down; you must be sitting up.

  Make sure that you *do not move your eyeballs* while you

are doing the "switch". You may have your eyes closed or open, you may blink, but you may not move your eyeballs to the left or right as you are performing the "switch". And you must be staring straight ahead of you. We actually demonstrate the *incorrect* way (obviously moving our eyeballs), and then the *correct* way.

You can imagine moving the container in any creative way that you like. For example, you can imagine it sliding from right to left (or vice versa) or that it jumps across the midline. You could imagine using some type of launcher to hurl it across or pretend that soldiers or gremlins carry it across. Or you could use a big bulldozer to push the container across to the other side. Use whatever method appeals to you.

Once the container is on the "other side" (but still in sight), you want to make it disappear. You can do this by imaging that it explodes, burns up, falls off a deep cliff or into the Bermuda Triangle, disintegrates magically, floats away, gets lasered, is sent off to burn up in the sun—however you want to imagine it.

We then wait for the client to complete this process. Once completed, we like briefly to take his mind off of the process by asking a totally unrelated question (such as where he bought some article of clothing he is wearing, if he ran into traffic on the way to the office, if he's comfortable going on to the next step, etc.). We call this a "break state," and we do it because we want to interrupt any residual feelings the client may be carrying over from the process he's just done. It also assists in making the last step a more precise test of whether or not the BRAIN-SWITCH has been effective. (If the client seems somehow curious about this change in subject, we explain that we asked something off-track to help pull him out of the feelings he'd been experiencing in creating his representations so we could move on to the next part of the process).

Step 6. Now imagine a positive container.

Now, on the *opposite* side of where you store your emotional memories (the side where you made the ugly container *disappear*), create in your imagination a container that you like. It could be a beautiful bowl or vase, a basket, a lovely antique trunk, a treasured jewelry box your grandmother gave you—any type of container that appeals to you. Or you could imagine a special object, such as a cross, a brooch, a service medal—any type of object that you value. It can be something you own, something you'd like to own, something you've seen in a store or in a magazine or online, or something purely from your imagination. The idea is to pick something that is precious to you and that you would treasure and never give away.

What you'll do in the next step is to imagine filling this positive container or object with thoughts/ideas/beliefs that you know to be true and that will assist you in keeping a good perspective the next time you think about mortar attacks.

We ask the client to describe the positive container or object he's chosen so that we can refer to it.

Step 7. Get positive thoughts/beliefs/understandings about the negative situation into your positive container.

When you think *logically* and *realistically* about the mortar attack(s), what do you know to be true about the experience(s) that are positive, resourceful thoughts? As you think of each realistic realization about the mortar attack(s), you will then imagine placing those thoughts—one by one—into your positive container. You can imagine them as "knowings and understandings", things that you know to be true or that you would tell a good friend about this situation.   These can take any form, for example, ideas written on paper or "bubbles of understanding" that get absorbed into the container.

Some clients prefer to imagine *themselves* as the container, with the "knowings and understandings" being assimilated into their essence.   Any creative way of imagining these understandings deposited into the positive container can be used.

I'm going to mention some resourceful thoughts now to give you the idea, but I don't want you to agree with me unless you really do agree. If you do agree, then I want you to imagine putting that thought into your positive container.

Examples might be as follows:

- It is perfectly normal to feel terrified during a mortar attack. You are not weak, crazy, or stupid because you were terrified. You are, in fact, smart, capable and thinking rationally.

- Given the circumstances, there was nothing you *realistically* could have done in the moments of the attack(s) to keep the people that died in the attack from being killed.

- Now that you are no longer in a war environment, sudden loud noises in your environment do not mean that you are being attacked by mortars.

As the client agrees with these statements—or modifies them in some way—we remind him to let that "bubble of understanding" be absorbed into his positive container or object. And we continue asking the client to think of any additional examples until he feels complete.

Step 8. The second "switch".

Now you're going to "switch" your positive container or object to the side where the ugly container was located originally, *placing it in the exact same spot where you had placed the original ugly container*—but with one important difference. Once you move it, *you're going to leave it there. You will not make it disappear.* When you think of this positive container or object in the future, you are unconsciously or consciously reminded of the "knowings and understandings" you placed in it. Remember, make sure when you do the "switch" that none of your body parts are crossed, that you stare straight ahead (eyelids open or closed), and that you do not move your eyeballs.

Step 9. Think about the original negative situation and notice how you feel.

Imagine a particular mortar attack. As you think of it now, how do you feel? If the BRAIN-SWITCH has been successful, the client should notice a positive difference. The original negative feeling in his body should not be present or be greatly diminished. He likely will feel calm or matter-of-fact as he recalls the event. We explain again that he will remember the event and the feelings he had about it, but he will no longer have the negative emotional and physical reactions.   He now has a realistic perspective about the situation and should no longer get triggered into a negative emotional or physical state.

As stated, most clients--after experiencing a BRAIN-SWITCH--report feeling lighter, calmer, or some positive feeling. But some may experience a period of disorientation, or their bodies may shake for several minutes to hours. If this happens, you'll want to reassure them that the above reactions are all normal, indicate that they have done some positive significant work, and need not be concerned.

We then ask the client not to discuss the BRAIN-SWITCH process with anyone for at least a week. Then they can tell anyone they wish, if they want to. We explain that we want the work they've just done to "rest and integrate", and we don't want them going over it in their own minds as they would have to do in order to explain the process to someone.

We also tell clients that we want to caution them about

something that probably won't happen, but if it does, we want them to know what to do. We'll say the following: **Suppose you wake up at three in the morning and think of something** *really important* **that you didn't think about while you were doing this process—something that should definitely have gone into that container you destroyed. If this should happen, all you have to do is get another ugly container (you don't bring back the one you destroyed; this is a new container although it can look exactly the same as the first one). Place images of the memory you forgot, whatever it is, into that container. Then perform the "switch", moving that container from your right to left** (or vice versa) **and then destroy it. Remember to sit up, don't cross any part of your body, and look straight ahead without moving your eyeballs when you do the switch. That's it. There's no need to do a second switch - you've already got your positive container with all the "knowings and understandings" that you have already put in place."**

Rarely do clients actually need this instruction, but if it becomes necessary, knowing what to do without having to wait for their next appointment keeps them from becoming unduly distressed about having "missed" something when they did their original "switch".

WHAT'S AHEAD

Now you've learned the basic elements of BRAIN-SWITCH. While it may seem complicated at this point, know that once you've done it a few times, it will become easy to remember. The next chapter will give you many examples of how we've used the process with our clients for a variety of issues.

PUTTING THE PROCESS TO WORK

We have found BRAIN-SWITCH to work very well in helping clients with a whole range of therapeutic issues, not just intensely traumatic ones. Clients have used the process to change limiting beliefs about themselves as well as to alter their reactions to negative events and emotions they have experienced. We have successfully treated clients who have issues stemming from rejection, criticism, abandonment and anger and find BRAIN-SWITCH helpful in clients who have depression, anxiety, self-esteem problems, phobias, test anxiety and other clinical problems.

To illustrate, this chapter consists of successful case studies taken from our practices where we have used the BRAIN-SWITCH process. We will include some cases of serious trauma as well as many other less traumatic issues that therapists treat. Of course, names and situational details have been changed to preserve anonymity.

We can typically remove trauma from *one* significant experience-- such as a rape or an instance of combat trauma--in one session. For example, our PTSD veterans who have terrifying nightmares that wake them up in a cold sweat (and sometimes fighting, so their spouses cannot sleep with them safely) usually can effectively process one nightmare about a combat experience in a session and, typically, not experience that same nightmare again. Many will have several recurring nightmares, requiring BRAIN-SWITCHES for each one. And some clients will require many BRAIN-SWITCHES, particularly those who have endured years of abuse growing up.

We've been able to follow up with some clients a year after their BRAIN-SWITCH experience and found that they have continued to be free from their original symptoms/issue. Others we have worked with over a several-month period because they have seen us for multiple issues, and they report the same success. So far, we know of only a few clients for which BRAIN-SWITCH did not work on the issue for which it was used.

Cassie

Cassie is an early-forties Iraq veteran who had served as a combat logistics officer and witnessed numerous disasters in her 9-month deployment. In one attack, over 61 people were injured or killed. Cassie's job was to assess all bodies to make sure there were no explosives on them. She had nightmares about that particular attack because of the enormity of the human casualties, the lack of resources to care for so many people at one time, her own exhaustion as she carried out her duties without sleep, and the grimness of her task.

Into her negative container, Cassie placed snapshots

representing the chaos and confusion during the attack, the calls of the wounded for help, and her searches of the dead bodies (and body parts). She also placed a snapshot of herself looking "dazed and robot-like" in her exhaustion. After the "switch", she put the following "bubbles of understanding" into the positive container:

- By finding several explosives during her body searches, she probably saved lives.

- Anyone would have felt exhausted and overwhelmed under the circumstances; she kept going in spite of it.

- Her unit was commended for their efficiency in dealing with the tragedy.

- She had been able to comfort a young terrified Iraqi child while a medic worked on the child's injuries, making Cassie feel that she had been of help on a personal level.

Megan

Megan was a 13-year-old Middle School student who had been bullied for several years by her classmates. She was creative and artistic, liking to make up stories and scripts. She had a movie star idol that she talked about often and collected posters and articles about the star. She was also a bit overweight. Her peers chided her about her "crazy stories", her weight, and for "being gay" (since her movie star idol was a female).

Megan filled her negative container with "snapshots" of her peers saying nasty things to her and then imagined burning the container to ashes. Into her positive container, she put the following "bubbles of understanding":

- Kids often make fun of anyone who is different in some way.

- Collecting memorabilia about a movie star of the same sex does not make one gay.

- She could lose about 10 pounds, but was certainly not fat.

- She got many kudos from teachers and other adults for her creativity.

- One day she would be an adult and would not have to hang out with anyone who put her down or said mean things about her unless she chose to do so.

- Her classmates might be jealous of her because she made good grades and was very smart.

Steve

Steve was an Iraq war veteran in his late thirties who had been in charge of training soldiers in his unit. One of his students with whom Steve felt a strong connection did not follow the standard procedure of locking down his weapon while not on duty. The student was standing with about three other soldiers talking casually with Steve when he accidentally dropped his weapon. The firearm discharged, the bullet entering the student's body just under his chin and through his head, killing him immediately and causing him to fall right at Steve's feet. Steve tried to revive the soldier, but was unsuccessful and the soldier died in Steve's arms. Steve was tormented by the feeling that he must have done something wrong during his training for the student to forget such an important instruction, and he had recurring nightmares about the event.

Into the negative container, Steve placed snapshots of the actual moment of the shooting, his attempts to save the solder's life, the soldier's funeral, and of Steve's giving instructions to his troops about the importance of locking down their weapons when not being attacked or on guard duty. Into the positive container, he placed the following "bubbles of understanding":

- He had definitely and repeatedly stressed safety instructions regarding weapons while training his soldiers.

- The combat medic in his unit had told him that there was no possible way the soldier's life could have been saved given the close-range shooting and the trajectory of the bullet.

- The solder had followed correct procedures about locking down his weapon numerous times prior to the accident; he definitely knew the correct procedure.

- The soldier's forgetting to lock down his weapon was just a simple human error with tragic consequences.

Mary Alice

Fifty-two-year-old Mary Alice was distressed because she could no longer visit her son, his wife, and their 3 teenagers in their home. Two of the teens got non-poisonous snakes as pets and also had an assortment of lizards. Mary Alice was petrified of the reptiles because at age five, she had found a snake coiled up in the spokes of her first bicycle and "freaked out" even at the thought of seeing a snake or reptile.

Mary Alice put into her negative container a picture of the snake entangled in her bicycle as well as several other situations in which she could not enter a pet shop that sold reptiles or occasions when she had "freaked out" when she had encountered a snake in an aquarium in school. She also represented herself on a vacation to Cancun, Mexico getting off a cruise ship and having to return to the ship, cancelling an excursion she was excited about, because she saw peddlers carrying iguanas on the beach.

Into the positive container she put the following "bubbles of understanding":

- There is good reason to stay away from snakes that are poisonous; however, she has never encountered a poisonous snake and did not live in an environment where seeing a poisonous snake was likely.

- Non-poisonous snakes do not harm or attack people.

- Her grandchildren's pet reptiles are non-poisonous, as are snakes sold in the typical pet store.

- Just because a reptile looks ugly—i.e. lizards—doesn't mean they are dangerous.

- Some snakes are beautifully patterned.

- She would never have to pick up or touch a snake or reptile unless she chose to.

After the BRAIN-SWITCH session, we asked Mary Alice to test the change on her way home by stopping in a pet store that sold reptiles. Thirty minutes later, she called to cheerfully report that snakes really do have beautiful patterns on their skins and that she had actually held a bearded lizard with no anxiety.

Maria

Maria, in her middle thirties, reported feeling "lost and confused" whenever she tried to make a point in an argument with her husband and he simply didn't understand or agree with her. Into her negative container, she put snapshots including a particularly difficult and emotional recent argument with her husband. Asked what else her unconscious knew should be in the container, she recalled coming home at age 10 and her mother telling her that her father had left the family, resulting in her feeling lost and confused for months. Then she added a snapshot of her boyfriend in high school breaking up with her, having no warning about or understanding of why he no longer wanted to be with her.

Into her positive container, Maria placed the following "bubbles of understanding":

- Her parents' divorce had nothing to do with Maria or with her lovability or worth.

- The longest she ever remained feeling lost and confused after an argument with her husband was about three hours, but most of the time, her upsetting feelings disappeared within a half hour or so.

- Most often her husband would apologize to her within a few hours after an argument, admitting that she had made a good point or had been right in her assessment of a situation.

- It is normal to feel confused and upset when someone you love leaves you and has given you no warning or explanation about their actions.

- She is a smart woman with many accomplishments and a family that loves her; there is no reason to feel "less than" just because someone she cares about doesn't agree with her.

- Everyone has times when they feel confused and/or irritated if they can't make another person understand their point of view.

Susan

Susan, in her early forties, had a vague memory that she had been sexually molested by her father at a young age. Even with hypnosis, she couldn't find an actual memory. She was very ambivalent about finding out what had happened and admitted that there was definitely a part of her that didn't want her to know.

We first did some work with the part of her that was so reluctant to let her know what happened and were able to get that part's agreement to proceed. Working with an "anxiety feeling" in her chest, she was able to remember instances of her father fondling her.

Susan made representations of various situations in which she remembered being fondled by her father as well as a collage of pictures of herself at various ages with that anxious feeling in her chest. She destroyed the container holding these images by imagining the negative container being struck by lightning and reduced to a twisted mass, which she then dropped into the Grand Canyon.

Her bubbles of understanding that she placed into her positive container included:

- Susan is a survivor.

- She is well liked and has a loving, caring husband and family.

- She received a "gift" resulting from the molestation: She is better able to help her daughter who was recently molested by a camp counselor.

- It was not her fault that her father chose to molest her.

Teresa

Teresa, in her late twenties, complained of depression and a lack of interest in activities she used to enjoy. She found it hard to get up and go to work in the mornings and described her life as "blah". This situation had been occurring since the death of her mother about 18 months before seeking treatment, with no prior history of depression. Discussion revealed that what really bothered her most was a fear that she would become demented and die in a fetal position as her mother had done.

Into her negative container Teresa put many pictures of her mother in various stages of deterioration over the three years that Teresa had cared for her. She made pictures of herself changing her mother's diapers, feeding her, and brushing her hair and teeth. She pictured her mother mistaking Teresa for one of her siblings and talking about how that sibling was always the favorite of her children.

Into her positive container she placed the following "bubbles of understanding":

- Her mother had numerous medical problems that likely contributed to her dementia. Teresa does not have any of those health issues.

- Her mother did not become demented until she was almost 90 years old.

- Her mother did love Teresa and knew that Teresa loved her.

- Teresa was a loving daughter to her mother throughout her mother's life.

Shaquille

Shaquille was an Afghanistan war veteran in his mid-twenties. He had been the driver of a Humvee that was hit by an IED, killing his gunner and blowing off both legs of his passenger. Shaquille received shrapnel wounds and numerous cuts on his body, but no life-threatening injuries. He was supposed to have been the gunner on that particular patrol, but the actual gunner did not want to drive that day and asked Shaquille to trade places with him. He had recurrent nightmares about this experience as well as survivor guilt.

Into the negative container Shaquille placed a video of the event as well as snapshots of unsuccessfully trying to revive the gunner, administering aid to his passenger, and carrying that soldier to a Medivac chopper. He put the following "bubbles of understanding" into the positive container:

- He had been instrumental in saving the life of his passenger.

- It was the gunner's idea for the two of them to trade places, not his.

- Being hit by an IED during a convoy is unpredictable in spite of soldiers being on alert to spot them. Tragically, it just happens.

Mark

Mark, a dentist in his mid-fifties, hired a new dental hygienist to work with him. She had been with him about a month but was driving him "crazy" because he found her voice tone to be highly irritating. In fact, he was considering firing her because he just couldn't stand her voice in spite of the fact that she was an excellent employee and the patients loved her. Mark made several images of the hygienist, hearing her annoying voice tone as she talked to him and to the patients.

Into his positive container Mark placed the following "bubbles of understanding":

- The hygienist is excellent at her job.

- Mark's patients really like the hygienist and have commented on her pleasing personality and gentle cleaning technique.

- Not one other person has complained about the hygienist's voice tone.

- Mark is really only around his hygienist for a very small percentage of his day.

When Mark returned to his office the next day, he called to leave a message that he couldn't understand what happened, but the hygienist's voice somehow didn't bother him at all (and the problem never returned).

Max

Max was a Vietnam veteran in his mid-sixties. Although very high functioning and compensating well for his PTSD, he had a terrifying nightmare that continued to haunt him and woke him up in a cold sweat several times a month. He dreamed that he is in a jungle at night and suddenly sees a large "evil, frightening green blob" that appears in the trees. The blob begins coming toward him and he awakens with a start, his heart pounding.

Into the negative container, Max put a picture of the green blob as well as several other snapshots of times he had spent frightening nights in a Vietnam jungle, always vigilant about Vietcong that could suddenly sneak up on him when he was on guard duty. Into his positive container Max put the following "bubbles of understanding":

- He survived the horrors of Vietnam.

- He is no longer in danger in his suburban home like he was during the war in Vietnam.

- It is normal to feel fear in such situations as he had experienced in Vietnam; it does not mean that he is a weak person.

A year later, Max has not had another nightmare about the green blob.

Kathy

Kathy, in her early twenties, was in sales and had a boss whose method of motivating his team was to use sarcasm and threats. He was also a hyper person who used excessive gesturing and movement when he gave a presentation. Kathy stated that her boss reminds her of "mean teenage boys" who used to make fun of her in high school and of the times she was teased for acting hyper when she was in elementary school.

Into her negative container Kathy placed videos of her boss giving presentations as well as snapshots of him making threatening and sarcastic remarks. She also made representations of herself being teased in high school for being hyper.

She put the following "bubbles of understanding" into her positive container:

- Her boss relates to everyone the same way; his behavior is not just directed toward Kathy.

- Her boss' sarcasm is not maliciously motivated.

- Kathy knows that in his heart, her boss is really supportive of her and wants her to succeed.

- Her boss' sarcastic remarks actually do prod Kathy to get her sales numbers up and thereby help her to succeed in spite of the way those remarks are delivered.

- Her boss is a very generous person and pays Kathy a salary that is higher than other sales people with similar experience.

Ellen

Ellen, in her early forties, was expecting a visit from her very critical mother later in the week. Her mother has always favored Ellen's younger sister, who could do no wrong in her mother's eyes. Ellen expected that her long weekend with her mother would be filled with negative comments about her and with bragging comments about her sister. She was particularly sensitive to her mother's jokingly calling her a "slut" when she wears shorts, and has a painful memory of her mother angrily calling her a "slut" when Ellen became pregnant at age 17 by her steady boyfriend of two years.

Into the negative container Ellen placed many examples of her mother criticizing her as well as examples where her mother seemed to clearly favor Ellen's sister. She included instances of her mother jokingly calling her a "slut" and, of course, included the painful time when her mother found out Ellen was pregnant and angrily called her a "slut".

Into the positive container Ellen put the following "bubbles of understanding":

- Her mother really does love Ellen but seems to be somewhat jealous of Ellen's accomplishments and attractive looks.

- Because Ellen had a wealthy father who was able to take her on wonderful vacations and buy her beautiful clothes—and her sister's father made a modest income—her mother's bragging about Ellen's sister is her mother's way of trying to compensate for her sister's never having had the advantages that can be provided by a wealthy father.

- Ellen's mother is a very insecure person and is highly judgmental and critical of everyone except Ellen's sister.

- Ellen feels genuinely sorry for her mother's unhappiness.

After her mother's visit, Ellen reported that all had gone well and her mother's critical remarks somehow didn't bother her.

Allison

Allison, age 17, was a star on her high school golf team and normally scored in the low 70's. For several months, she had not been getting along with her teammates ("so much drama") and her game had worsened as a result. Into the negative container, she placed audio recordings of her team members' catty remarks and snapshots of their dirty looks when Allison scored well.

Into the positive container Allison placed the following "bubbles of understanding":

- Allison is going to be friendlier and less stand-offish to her teammates.

- She will remain positive and upbeat, detaching herself from the "drama" without detaching herself from team.

- She will work with her therapist to learn an "anchoring" process to help her focus and perform at her best.

- She will become a better team member by supporting her teammates and acknowledging their successes and improvements.

Allison went back to shooting her former excellent scores and won a golf tournament.

Cecily

Cecily, in her late thirties, had been date-raped by a boyfriend in high school. Although she had talked about the rape during a brief psychiatric hospitalization in her early twenties, the memory of the rape intruded into her consciousness often and left her tearful and with uncomfortable bodily sensations (tightness in chest, lump in throat).

Into her negative container, Cecily made a video of the rape, of her scrubbing herself in a very long shower afterward, and of her being vigilant about not running into the ex-boyfriend in school (even hiding in a restroom to avoid passing him in the hall). Into her positive container Cecily put the following "bubbles of understanding":

- Cecily was adamant about saying "No" repeatedly to her boyfriend (rather than passively submitting to him), which was a courageous act.

- The fact that she didn't tell anyone about the rape until years later is typical of date-rape victims, so she need not feel guilty about it.

- "Making out" with a boy" does not give him permission to force a girl into having sex.

- The event did not ruin her life, as she had feared. She is happily married with two well-adjusted children, has many friends, and is a respected volunteer in her community.

Elaine

Elaine, in her mid-twenties, was worried about not sleeping. About a month prior, she and her husband had acquired a puppy and Elaine had gotten up with it every hour through the night to take it outside to housebreak it. This resulted in about 4 days of sleep deprivation for her during which time she became overwhelmed and exhausted. Her doctor gave her some sleep medication that she took once, sleeping well for the next 10 days. On the 11th day, the night before her mother and brother were flying in for a visit, she was very excited in anticipation of the visit and could not fall asleep immediately. She began to panic, anticipating a night without any sleep which then made her anxious through the entire night until she finally took her sleep medication at 6 AM and slept for 6 hours. Now she worries obsessively during the day that she will not be able to sleep that night.

Into her negative container Elaine placed snapshots representing the 4-day period of "freaking out" with sleep deprivation and of her tossing and turning the night before her relatives' visit. She also placed several snapshots of herself having chest pains while driving about 6 months prior as well as visits to several doctors during which she was reassured that there was nothing wrong with her heart. Into her positive container she placed the following "bubbles of understanding":

- It is normal to feel "freaked out" and exhausted if a person has not slept in four days.

- It is not unusual for people to have some difficulty falling asleep when they are excited about an upcoming event the next day, but she had catastrophized the situation by telling herself that she was not going to be able to sleep the entire night and would end up like she did when she was sleep deprived for four days.

- It is normal to feel anxious if you experience chest pain, and she did the right thing in checking it out with her doctors to rule out a medical condition.

- She had slept very well and without medication for 10 days after her sleep deprivation experience as well as the few nights since her relatives' visit.

Elaine noticed when doing the second part of the BRAIN-SWITCH that her positive container "had to be forced to the other side" and was resisting. Exploration of this revealed that there was part of Elaine that wanted to continue having the sleep problem because she had been missing her family and they were now in contact with her more often to make sure she was okay. After deciding that it was practical for her and her family to plan visits about every three months, that she would begin texting her family to keep in better touch with them, and that she would skype during their weekly phone calls, Elaine was able to complete the second part of the BRAIN-SWITCH with no problem. In a follow-up a month later, she reported that she had not been having any difficulty sleeping.

Roberto

Roberto, in his late thirties, had an upsetting memory of being chased as a young boy by a pack of wild dogs, barely escaping. Whenever something went wrong in his life, he would go back to this experience, stating that it had been the beginning of his feelings of being a victim. He had tried to keep himself from becoming victimized by constantly trying to please others and was often taken advantage of as a result. His family had moved to the United States from Mexico when Roberto was 10 and spoke no English. He was made fun of by other children in school as he struggled to learn the new language. His first wife had alienated his three children from him and he had no relationship with them, a situation that bothered him a great deal. His current wife was divorcing him against his will because he was not a good enough provider even though he had a trade and had always worked full-time. All of these experiences culminated in his feeling unworthy and defeated. He stated that "being chased by dogs" was a metaphor for his life.

Into the negative container, Roberto placed approximately 25 snapshots of all these events. He then placed the following "bubbles of understanding" into his positive container:

- Roberto is indeed a survivor — both from the dogs that chased him as well as the children that teased him.

- Children are known to be cruel to those who are "different" in some way.

- The dogs that chased Roberto resulted from his being in the wrong place at the wrong time; this would have happened to any person who found himself in that same situation and says nothing about Roberto's worth as a person.

- Roberto now speaks fluent English, is well respected for his craft and has a very close relationship with his two children from his second marriage. He does not have to see himself as a victim.

Jeremy

Jeremy, in his early forties, had been having anxiety symptoms that date back a few months to the death of his dog. He had punished the dog for pooping on the living room carpet (the dog was totally trained) and sternly put him in his crate for punishment. Jeremy maintained that he had never been abusive to the dog but, due to his temper, was "rough" with his pet as he disciplined him. Later that evening, it became clear that the dog was ill. The dog died during the night, with both Jeremy and his wife petting and comforting him in his last hours. When he took his dog to a veterinarian to be cremated, he was told that it had died of a ruptured spleen.

In the negative container Jeremy placed snapshots of his roughly shoving his dog into a crate as well as several images of the dog's last few hours and the conversation with the veterinarian. Into the positive container, he placed the following "bubbles of understanding":

- Jeremy knows that he loved his dog dearly, that the dog knew he was loved, and that he and his dog had had many wonderful times together.

- There were no signs that his dog was hurt or ill in any way when Jeremy put him in the crate.

- If he had known the dog was ill, he would not have disciplined him for pooping on the carpet.

- Jeremy never had any intent to hurt his dog.

- Jeremy would work with his therapist to understand the origins of his anger as well as techniques for managing it.

Helen

Helen, age forty, was very worried about an upcoming dental procedure. When going to the dentist in the past, she would start shaking and crying even when there was no pain involved. This behavior made her feel embarrassed and "crazy". She had realized that her position in a dentist's chair was similar to the position her father had placed her in when he sexually abused her when she was young, and that her father always came into her bed from the right side—just as the dentist always approaches a patient from the right side.

Into her negative container Helen placed images of her father entering her bed from the right side and sexually abusing her. She also imaged a collage of her past experiences at the dentist where she would shake and cry even when nothing uncomfortable was happening. Into her positive container she placed the following "bubbles of understanding":

- The dentist has no intention of sexually abusing her. She has gone to him for years and knows he is a safe person.

- When Helen was a little girl, she was powerless to stop her father from sexually abusing her. Now she is an adult, and if a dentist (or anyone else) made inappropriate advances to her she would get up and leave immediately.

Helen reported that her next dental appointment went well; she felt comfortable and did not shake or cry.

Melanie

Melanie was in her early thirties and very critical of herself. Her history revealed that she had a limiting belief: "I'm not good enough." When she was growing up, her father was an alcoholic who was verbally abusive both to Melanie and to her mother, and her mother had periods of depression during which she stayed in her room and did not interact much with Melanie. Melanie tried to "take care of things at home" to keep her father from getting angry and to help her mother out with the household chores. But she couldn't "fix" her mother or her father, telling herself that she just must not be good enough.

Into the negative container Melanie put snapshots of her father's drunken verbal rages and her mother's lying on the couch or staying in bed most of the day. She also made pictures of times she had made some mistake, such as forgetting to put the dog out, having a messy room, or turning in a wrong assignment in school. She pictured getting a rejection letter from her first-choice college, overhearing mean remarks about her from a boy she had a crush on, and being overlooked for a promotion at work.

Into her positive container Melanie put the following

"bubbles of understanding":

- Her parents behaved the way they did because of their own childhood and life experiences and their level of emotional health and maturity (or lack of it).

- She could have been any little girl in that family and her parents would have responded the same way; their behavior had nothing to do with her worth or lovability.

- In spite of her parents' less-than-perfect parenting, Melanie knows that they both love her and are proud of her.

- Everybody makes mistakes and has disappointments; it does not mean they are not "good enough" or have something wrong with them.

- Melanie has many successes: She is happily married, has good friends, is a gourmet cook, and enjoys her career as a journalist.

Nora

Nora, now in her late thirties, had been raped at knifepoint while walking through a park on her way to school as a foreign exchange college student in another country. She had fought her attacker and still has scars from the knife blade on one of her thighs. When she got to the school after her attacker fled, the school secretary said, "You should know better than to walk through that park!" Then when she was taken to the hospital, the person who needed to examine her was not there. She was told to return the next day but not to bathe or "clean herself up", adding to her trauma.

Now years later, she continues to have a feeling in the pit of her stomach that "something bad is going to happen to me".

Into her negative container Nora put a video of the rape and snapshots of her experiences afterward both at the school as well as at the hospital. She also included snapshots of times she has felt scared about being attacked or having something bad happen to her. Into her positive container, she put the following "bubbles of understanding":

- She is very grateful that she survived the attack and proud of the fact that she did try to stop her attacker to the best of her ability and probably saved her own life.

- Nobody had warned her about the danger of the park where she was raped; she was not being careless or irresponsible by walking through that park in the daytime.

- Many rape victims experience further trauma in the way they are treated by people when they report that they have been raped.

- Her rape experience has allowed her to be more empathetic to people who have suffered various kinds of trauma.

- She is proud that she finished her semester abroad and went on to successfully complete her degree.

Damian

Damian is a late-twenties Iraq war veteran who spent his entire

10-month deployment as a combat medic. He had many symptoms of PTSD but was particularly bothered by nightmares of his war experiences, which interrupted his sleep. He dreams about the soldiers he cared for who he knew were not going to live, yet he had to assure them they were going to be okay. He also dreams about Iraqi children who died in his arms when he was trying to help them, and about one particular buddy who was dying and asked Damian to visit his wife and son after Damian returned to the States (he had not had the money to do so).

Damian made images of all these situations as well as snapshots of being without sleep for 36 hours, exhausted as he cared for a large number of seriously wounded soldiers who had been ambushed. Into his positive container, he put the following "bubbles of understanding":

- He actually was responsible for saving many lives during his time as a medic.

- He made the decision to contact his buddy's wife by skype and talk with her.

- People die in wars even though they get the best care that is available on a battlefield. It was not his fault that they died.

- He believed it was the right thing to do to try to comfort soldiers by giving them hope even if he did know they would die.

Wendy

Wendy was in her mid-forties, a high-functioning survivor of a long history of repeated sexual and physical abuse by both parents until she left home at age 18. Her therapy had included dozens of BRAIN-SWITCH processes. One involved her body image. She had been an excellent gymnast in her teens, but gained about 60 pounds after she married and had children. Although she had lost all of her extra weight years before coming to therapy, she continued to see herself as "fat and unattractive".

Into Wendy's negative container she placed pictures of herself in various situations when she was overweight as well as snapshots of herself as a gymnast when her food intake and weight were constantly monitored by her coach and her parents. Rather than using a positive container, she put a recent picture of herself along with the following "bubbles of understanding":

- As she imagines herself turning 360 degrees in the current picture of herself, she notices all the places that she used to carry extra fat and now sees a trim figure.

- She has worn a size 4 "petite" for many years.

- She can now be attractive and trim without worry of being sexually abused.

Wendy reported that after her therapy session, she spent the afternoon lying out by a swimming pool. She kept falling asleep, but awakened every 30 minutes or so. Each time she woke up, she noticed her arms, legs and stomach looked smaller. After several instances of waking up, she actually saw herself for the first time with the petite body that she truly has.

Walter

Walter, in his mid-sixties, could not drive on a freeway. About eight months prior, he had been involved in an accident where a semi-- going in the opposite direction--had crossed over the midline and hit his car and the boat he was towing. He and his wife ended up with their car on the right shoulder, fortunately unhurt, but his boat was totaled. Since the accident, Walter was extremely nervous when driving. Whenever a large vehicle was approaching, even on a four-lane highway, Walter would pull over to the right shoulder and stop until that vehicle had passed.

Into his negative container Walter placed a video of the accident. He also included snapshots of himself driving nervously and stopping on the right shoulder when a large vehicle was approaching in the opposite lane. Into his positive container, he placed the following "bubbles of understanding":

- He has had numerous semis and large vehicles pass him going the opposite way for 50 years with no problems; this accident was highly unusual and unlikely to be repeated.

- Walter had responded well under the circumstances, guiding his car safely to the road shoulder.

- Walter understands he is a good driver and has avoided several would-be accidents because of his driving skills.

- People have been known to slip and fall in a bathtub and die, but we don't stop taking baths. Walter would find it very inconvenient not to drive on freeways, and the odds of that type of accident happening again to him were extremely low.

- Pulling to the shoulder of the road every time he sees a large vehicle coming toward him is much more likely to cause an accident than staying on his regular route.

Walter resumed his normal driving after the BRAIN-SWITCH with no problems.

Sienna

Sienna, in her mid-thirties, was facing surgery and was petrified. A few years prior, she had had an operation during which she had experienced the terror of being paralyzed and unable to speak for about 30 seconds when the technicians in the operating room thought she was anesthetized. This memory also triggered her to remember times as a pre-school child when she had been physically tortured by a psychotic mother who would enter Sienna's bedroom at night and "stick things" in her bladder to punish Sienna for wetting her pants.

Into her negative container, Sienna placed images of the operating room scene where she had become paralyzed as well as pictures of her mother's painful torturing of her. Her "bubbles of understanding" in the positive container included:

- The medical personnel in the operating room where she would have surgery had no intent to torture or hurt her; rather, they were there to take care of a necessary medical procedure which would help her feel better.

- The surgery she was going to have is a structured procedure; she knew what to expect and what would be done. With her mother, part of her terror was that there was no structure and she never knew what to expect or what else her mother might do to her.

- She had talked with the anesthesiologist who was to be present during her surgery, told him what had happened in her last surgery, and he had reassured her that he had a way to monitor her closely to know if she was really asleep before the process began.

- She liked and trusted her doctors; this made her feel safe going into the surgery.

Sienna was able to go through her surgery without experiencing any trauma.

****

Now you've seen a number of problems to which we've applied the BRAIN-SWITCH process. However, it is not limited just to these kinds of issues. We and our colleagues continue on a daily basis to find new situations where BRAIN-SWITCH is applicable.

WHAT IF YOU GET STUCK?

Now let's take a look at what can go wrong during the BRAIN-SHIFT process—and how to fix it!

The Client Reports No Difference In Feeling Between The Right And Left Images (Sounds)

Typically, when you ask a client to make an image of an emotionally upsetting experience, she will easily be able to tell you what she is feeling in her body as she thinks of it. If you ask her to take that image (sound) and move it to the opposite side of her "mind's eye", she will notice that the feelings disappear or lessen considerably. One side, either left or right, is more "emotional". But some clients do not report any difference; they report that they feel the emotions equally on both sides—or feel no particular emotion on either side.

Give the client an eye patch and ask her to place the patch over one eye and then tell you about the negative experience. We suggest putting the patch over the left eye first since the majority of people have their right side as the more emotional side. Assuming this is true, the client should readily access her emotions. If she relates the experience calmly and without emotion, then have her switch the patch to the right eye.

By switching the sides of the patch back and forth, it should become clear which side produces the emotions for that client.

The Client Becomes So Flooded With Emotion That She Cannot Talk About Her Experience

Some clients become overwhelmed with their emotions and cannot get the necessary distance from the experience to be able to talk about it. An example would be a woman who had been raped and, when asked to begin making mental pictures of the rape for the BRAIN-SWITCH process, begins sobbing, shaking, and unable to relay the information.

When this happens, our goal is to get the client to dissociate from her experience. There are several ways we use to accomplish this:

We ask the client simply to imagine that she is watching the traumatic event from a distance. For example, she is sitting in a theater and watching a brief film or video clip of the trauma on the screen (single dissociation). If the client is still experiencing such strong emotion that she cannot talk about the experience, we ask her to step further back in the theater and watch herself watching the film of the traumatic event that she sees on the screen.

Another method is to ask the client while she is being very emotional to tell us the age that she *feels* she is as she experiences the strong emotion. Typically, she will say that she feels she is acting the age she actually was when the trauma happened. To get her fully into the experience, we ask her questions like **"Where are you?"** If she says, "In my house", we then ask, **"What room are you in?" "Who else is there?" What is the surface beneath you?" "Is it soft or hard?" "What do you see, taste, smell?"** In other words, we want the client to get fully into the experience of where the trauma occurred.

Next, we tell her **"Now we want you to leave that 5-year-old (or whatever age) in that chair—and we want you, the adult she became, to move over to this chair** (usually, the therapist's chair). Once the client has settled into the new chair, we ask **"Now, tell us what happened to that little girl so long ago (in that situation, when she was 5, etc)."**

If the client is unable to dissociate enough to be able to talk about her traumatic experience, we will use a third, more elaborate, method similar to a neurolinguistic programming technique known as the Fast Phobia Cure. To do this, we ask her to imagine that she is in a movie theater - with or without the therapist beside her, her choice - and that nobody else can enter that theater. We ask her to imagine taking a seat in the theater, describing where she prefers to sit, noticing the color of the upholstery, whether the seat has a cup holder and whether it slides. We ask her to notice that there is a blank screen in the front, at some distance from her. We mention all these things because we want her to immerse herself as much as possible in the feeling of being in a theater.

We then ask her to imagine that she could magically leave

her body in the theater seat and float *up and back* into the projection booth. We ask her to take a seat in the booth, imagining any type and color of comfortable chair she would like to have in that booth, possibly a swivel chair. Then we ask her to imagine that she can look down into the theater and see the back of her head and shoulders (and perhaps ours as well) - and then to notice how much further away the blank screen is now from her perspective in the booth. Again, we want her to vividly imagine being in a projection booth. We remind her that she is totally safe in our office as she is imagining these things.

Then we instruct her: **"In a moment, I'm going to ask you to see on the screen a brief movie showing the rape. You will begin the film at a point where you felt safe just before it started and end the film at the point where you felt safe again, perhaps back at your home. You will just take a few seconds to run the film - like when you fast-forward something on your television - and the film will be in black and white. Remember to make the whole thing just a few seconds long. Any questions? Ready, begin."** From this dissociated position, she should be able to imagine the rape scene without so much emotion.

When the client finishes the film clip, we continue: **"Now I'm going to describe something but don't want you to do it until I tell you you're ready to do it. You're going to imagine that you can float out of the projection booth, pick up your body in the theater and then float to the screen. Then you're going to run the exact same film clip you just ran - but with these differences. The film will be in color and you're going to run it *backwards* from** the point where you knew you were safe after the rape to the point where you felt safe before the rape ever started. **You can even hear the sound of the film going backwards** (we make the sound to illustrate). **And you're going to imagine that you are actually *in the film* as though you are being sucked backwards. In other words, you're not going to imagine *seeing yourself*, but imagine that you are *actually in the film*. And the whole thing will be very fast in the time it takes to say "whoosh" (about 2 seconds)."**

After clarifying any questions from the client, we say **"Okay, now imagine that you're leaving the projection booth and floating down into the theater to collect your body. And now you float up on the screen ready to be in the film as it runs backwards, hearing the sound, in color, very fast. Ready? Begin."**

When the client finishes running the film clip, we ask her to run the same clip (backwards and in color) about 5-10 more times, going faster each time. We ask her to close her eyes to run the clips, opening them for a brief second after completing each one. As she begins running each clip, we say **"Faster! Faster!"** until she is just blinking rapidly. At that point, the process is over and we ask the client just to relax. She should now be able to do the BRAIN-SWITCH on the rape experience with much less emotional distress.

The objective with all three of these techniques is to give the client some distance from the emotions of the trauma so that she is able to relate what happened to her.

We often find that clients, particularly combat veterans, will tell us that they can't get the "ugly" container to move to the opposite side (or it keeps popping back into its original place after they've moved it) or they cannot destroy the container (or after they do, it pops back). What this means is that some part of the client wants to hold on to the negative emotions from his traumatic experience. A big part of him, of course, wants to stop suffering; but there is another part, typically unconscious, that wants the suffering to continue.

Clients, when we break this news to them, typically think this is a crazy idea. But therapists know that the part of the client that wants them to continue the suffering really is trying to help the client in some way; that part has a positive *intention* even though it also keeps the client feeling miserable. To tease out the positive intention, we ask the client, **"What bad thing might happen if you were able to stop feeling the anger (fear, guilt, shame, etc.) over this experience?" "How would your life change if this experience no longer continues to haunt you?" "How is keeping this memory alive protecting you?"**

Here are some examples:

- Bob knows that his anger over having to do things that went against his conscience when he was in Iraq makes him irritable and explosive, playing havoc with his relationship with his wife and children. But a part of him is afraid to give up the anger; he believes it is his anger that has motivated him to accomplish things. Without the anger, he fears that he will be unmotivated and not reach the goals he sets for himself.

- Rebecca believes that she needs to continue being hypervigilant about passing items located on or near the edge of the road while she is driving. She thinks that if she becomes relaxed when she is driving past a dead animal, a discarded tire, a box or a bag in or near the road, her car will blow up. The part of her that wants her to continue being anxious is trying to protect her from being harmed.

- Juan has a part that doesn't want him to destroy the "ugly" container that is filled with grim images of battle torn bodies and body parts that he had to retrieve and place in body bags. That part feels that it dishonors the memory of the dead soldiers to "blow them up again" or destroy them in some unceremonious manner. He wanted to "bury them with the honor and respect they deserved". Rather than destroying the container in the usual ways, he decided to make the container a silver coffin and then, when moving it to the other side, envisioned a military burial complete with a 21 gun salute.

- Roland cannot destroy his "ugly" container; it keeps re-appearing even after he tries to burn it. A part of him believes that he should continue to suffer because of survivor guilt. Since he didn't die or lose a limb—and his buddies did—a part of him believes that he does not deserve to be at peace or have happiness in his life.

So how does a therapist get around these blocks? A method

we use involves four steps:

1. We find the positive intention of the part of the client that wants that person to keep the problem as described above.

2. We begin a "conversation" with that part by stating **"We want to talk now to that part of you that wants you to continue feeling 'x' (the negative feeling)."** Then we ask that part, **"If we could find another way that your positive intention could be met without (client's name) having to continue to suffer 'x', would you be willing to rely on those other methods, knowing that if they don't work, you can always go to back to making (client's name) suffer 'x'?"** Typically, the part will agree.

3. We then ask the client to brainstorm answers to this question: **"What other ways do you have of meeting that positive intention without having to resort to 'x'?"** The client then must come up with at least one acceptable answer.

4. We ask the part with the positive intention if it agrees that the solution the client has generated is acceptable and, when the part agrees, we ask if it is ready now to allow the other method of ensuring that the positive intention is met, eliminating the need for "x". If the part does not agree, then more brainstorming needs to occur until an acceptable solution is found.

Some examples will make this clearer:

- William was infuriated by his military Commander who was

prejudiced against William's race and repeatedly gave William the "dirty jobs". In doing the BRAIN-SWITCH process, William's container with all the negative representations of all the times he'd been discriminated against would not move to the other side of the midline. "It's like there's a wall blocking me," he stated. In establishing the positive intention of the part of William that did not want him to stop being angry about his mistreatment, he said "I guess I'm afraid that if I stop being so angry, I just won't accomplish things. My anger has allowed me to be successful."

Asked to brainstorm how else he could know that he would be successful even if he wasn't angry, he said, "I have always been a highly motivated person, even before the discrimination experience; I always set goals for myself and then follow up, even when I'm not angry." With this realization, he was able to complete the BRAIN-SWITCH process.

- During BRAIN-SWITCH Bryan could not "move over" his container filled with memories about retrieving dead bodies from the battlefield. We asked him to consider that he had a part of him that did not want to let go of his anguish over this, and *that part of him* had some positive intention in keeping him tormented. Asking, **"What bad thing might happen if you no longer anguished over this?"** he stated, "Well, I don't feel that I am honoring those dead soldiers' memories if I don't continue thinking about it all the time." We then asked him to brainstorm other ways that he could make sure he honored those dead soldiers. He came up with "I will attend a Memorial Day service and say a prayer for them every Memorial Day." For Bryan, this solution made sense to him, and he was then able to successfully move the container with the dead bodies across the midline and destroy it during the BRAIN-SWITCH process.

Note: If you are familiar with NLP, you may recognize this process as similar to the "Six Step Reframe".

The Switch Didn't Work

We have had a couple of instances where clients have reported that the BRAIN-SWITCH didn't work. Either they continued to have strong emotional feelings during the "check" immediately after doing the process, or they reported weeks later that they continue to be triggered by the traumatic event.

When a client reports during the "check" that they still experience the negative emotions when they think about images of a trauma that they've just "moved over", questioning usually reveals that they had some problem during the process that they did not disclose. They either couldn't move the container with the negative images across the midline (from right to left, or vice versa) or they report problems destroying the container. In either case, refer to the above methods for dealing with these issues.

If clients tell us at a later session that they are still triggered by their traumatic events, we ask **"So what message might your unconscious be sending you about this?"** For example, occasionally a combat veteran stops having nightmares about the trauma for weeks or months, but then suddenly it reappears. Typically the veteran has been re-triggered in some new way.

Perhaps he saw a movie in which a similar trauma to his occurred, or he talked to another veteran who described the same traumatic situation in detail. Or maybe he thought of another important event related to the original trauma that he did not put into the container that was destroyed during the first BRAIN-SWITCH process of that trauma.

When this happens, we ask the client to do another BRAIN-SWITCH process *on the event that re-triggered him.* In other words, he will take the new nightmare (or the incident where his buddy told him about a similar traumatic event, or the new awareness of another incident that should have gone into the container when it was originally destroyed), make a representation of that nightmare or incident, put the image in *another* container, move that container to the opposite side (right or left) and then destroy it.

It is important that the client knows not to retrieve the *original container.* That one is gone for good. The new container may look just like the one that was destroyed, but it is a *new* container. Containers that have been destroyed by a BRAIN-SWITCH process are never brought back.

FINAL THOUGHTS

***While BRAIN-SWITCH is a powerful process and has a structure, it is important to note that—as in any therapeutic tool—the level of experience and creativity of the therapist who uses it is critically important for success. For example, there are times when it is not necessary to use the "positive" container switch. Yet there are no hard and fast rules about this; it depends on the therapist's intuition. And there are times when instructions have to be modified to fit a particular client's situation (such as when the veteran felt it would be "highly disrespectful" to destroy the negative container holding body bags but, at the therapist's suggestion, was satisfied with using a silver coffin as the container and simply burying it with a 21 gun salute). The therapist's intuitive understanding of the client's issue plus flexibility and creativity in using the tool takes precedence over a rigid application of the process.

***We have found it helpful as therapists to use the BRAIN-SWITCH process on ourselves after a particularly upsetting session. Sometimes clients describe horrific, gruesome events which can be difficult for the therapist not to think about after a session is over.

Making a very brief video of the session and "switching" it prevents us from taking those awful images home with us!

APPENDIX A

Joseph LeDoux PhD, Neuroscientist and Psychologist, Director of The Emotional Brain Institute (EBI) of the <u>Center for Neural Science at NYU</u>, is a world renowned researcher in the study of the brain mechanisms of emotion. His books, <u>*The Emotional Brain*</u> and <u>*Synaptic Self*</u>, have been translated into numerous languages and are used to guide researchers and clinicians in their efforts to understand and treat emotions. His work at the EBI aims to build on his past groundbreaking research using animal models to unlock the secrets of emotions, especially fear and anxiety. Fear and anxiety are of interest on their own, but also contribute to common psychiatric disorders across the lifespan. Dr. LeDoux is a University Professor, Henry and Lucy Moses Professor of Science, and Professor of Neural Science and Psychology at NYU.

Anxiety and fear are normal responses to threatening events. However, when fear and anxiety are expressed beyond the extent called for by the situation, an anxiety disorder exists. More than 40 million Americans suffer from anxiety disorders, at a cost of more than $50 billion per year. Because anxiety disorders do not necessarily remove people from their societal roles, anxious children often remain in schools and anxious adults remain in the workforce, both in compromised states.

Anxiety also makes depression, schizophrenia, autism, mental retardation, eating disorders, and drug addiction worse by facilitating worry and causing memory and attention deficits. In addition, it can exacerbate the effects of other medical problems such as cancer or heart disease by potentiating the effects of stress and compromising immune reactions.

According to Dr. LeDoux's research, negative emotions such as fear and anxiety are the root of human suffering. These emotions impair memory, attention, decision-making and creativity, and inhibit social behavior. Moreover, early stress and anxiety make it harder to regulate emotions later in life. Through better understanding of emotional systems, EBI researchers hope to identify ways to retrain the brain to inhibit negative emotions and thereby release these other systems from the tyranny of anxiety. The development of such evidence-based treatment will have far-reaching implications.

From "Opinionator" Blog in the New York Times, (2012)

APPENDIX B

On the next pages you will see a tool we find helpful in documenting the client's severity of PTSD symptoms. We then find it useful to give the assessment periodically (so long as the client remains in therapy) to assess progress.

PTSD CLIENT QUESTIONNAIRE

Name: _____ Date: _____

(please circle your best answer)

SLEEP PROBLEMS:

I have nightmares:
nightly   4-6x week   1-3x week   less than 1x a week   a couple
a month   every few months   none

Average time to fall asleep:
under 30 min   30-60 minutes   60-120 minutes   more than 120 min

I wake up an average of:
once or twice a night   3-4 times a night   more than 5 x a night

I sleep an average of _____ hours a night.

PTSD SYMPTOMS:
(0 = not at all, 1-5 = low occurrence; 6-10 is high occurrence)

Recurrent & distressing recollections of the event(s).
　　　0 1 2 3 4 5 6 7 8 9 10

Recurrent distressing dreams of the event(s).
　　　0 1 2 3 4 5 6 7 8 9 10

Acting or feeling as if the event(s) are reoccurring (flashbacks;
including those that occur on awakening or when intoxicated).
　　　0 1 2 3 4 5 6 7 8 9 10

Intense psychological distress at exposure to internal or external cues that symbolize or resemble an aspect of the traumatic event(s).

0 1 2 3 4 5 6 7 8 9 10

Physiological reactivity on exposure to internal or external cues that symbolize or resemble an aspect of the traumatic event(s).

0 1 2 3 4 5 6 7 8 9 10

Efforts to avoid thoughts, feelings, or conversations associated with the trauma.

0 1 2 3 4 5 6 7 8 9 10

Efforts to avoid activities, places, or people that arouse recollections of the trauma.

0 1 2 3 4 5 6 7 8 9 10

Inability to recall an important aspect of the trauma(s).

0 1 2 3 4 5 6 7 8 9 10

Markedly diminished interest or participation in significant activities.

0 1 2 3 4 5 6 7 8 9 10

Feeling of detachment or estrangement from others.

0 1 2 3 4 5 6 7 8 9 10

Restricted range of affect (e.g., unable to have loving feelings).

0 1 2 3 4 5 6 7 8 9 10

Sense of a foreshortened future (e.g. does not expect to have a career, marriage, children, or a normal life span).

0 1 2 3 4 5 6 7 8 9 10

Irritability or outbursts of anger.

0 1 2 3 4 5 6 7 8 9 10

Difficulty concentrating.

0 1 2 3 4 5 6 7 8 9 10

Hypervigilance.

0 1 2 3 4 5 6 7 8 9 10

Exaggerated startle response.

0 1 2 3 4 5 6 7 8 9 10

Guilt.

0 1 2 3 4 5 6 7 8 9 10

Acknowledgments

There are a number of people I would like to thank for their ideas and contributions.

Foremost is my co-author Judi Craig, Ph.D. who was the driving force behind translating my ideas to paper. Not only did Judi actually write most of the book, but also as a psychotherapist working daily with clients, she has probably used BRAIN-SWITCH more than any other therapist and her insights pervade this work.

I would also like to thank Fred Brown, M.D., Harry Lundell, M.A., LPC, and Rosemary Stauber, Ph.D. for their feedback and suggestions in refining the BRAIN-SWITCH process. Many thanks also to Marilyn and Al Sargent for their initial insights about the differing experience that occurs in each eye. Al established that when people see things out of their right eye only, they show more feeling/emotion, whereas when they look out of their left eye only, they tend to see things with more objectivity. (I refer you to Al's book The Other Mind's Eye).

My enduring thanks to Carl Buchheit, Ph.D and Carla Camus for introducing me to the eye patch phenomena and the remarkable differences that occurred when one eye vs. the other was covered. And to my dear friend, Jim Norris for his encouragement when I had the process of BRAIN-SWITCH refined but just didn't think the book could happen.

Although he doesn't know it, I owe a big thank you to Joseph

LeDoux, Ph.D., for his lecture in San Antonio. Dr. LeDoux presented data from his lab indicating the amygdala is intrinsically involved in creating and remembering trauma. I realized whatever change was made as the internal imaging shifted also modified the amygdala's reaction. For me, his research both confirmed that BRAIN-SWITCH works and explained *why* it works.

I'd also like to acknowledge the founders and co-founders of NLP for recognizing the power of our images and self-talk in determining our patterns of thought and behavior.

And the biggest influence of all was my wife of 10 years, Carol, my best friend and sounding board for the discoveries I made as this technique coalesced. Her belief in me was unwavering as I pieced together the elements of what ultimately became BRAIN-SWITCH.

Jonathan (July 2012)

****

I wish first to express my deep gratitude to my clients who have entrusted me with their painful memories. As I have listened to their struggles - and their courage in facing them - I have felt privileged to be a part of their healing.

I also wish to acknowledge the brilliance of my co-author, Jonathan, in creating the BRAIN-SWITCH process. As my Mentor and friend, I consistently admire his intellectual curiosity, his creativity, his compassion, and his ability to think "outside the box". I deeply thank him for the honor of co-authoring his book.

Additionally, we are very grateful for Domenic Fusco

(www.imageartistry.com) who brought his wonderful creativity to our cover design and helped us greatly with all the "computer stuff" involved in creating the book.

Lastly, I'd like to thank Jonathan's wife, Carol, for her superb editing skills as well as my friend and colleague Rosemary Stauber, Ph.D. for her helpful feedback. And, of course, my husband, Jim Norris, for his never-ending support - and for keeping me laughing.

Judi (July 2012)

REFERENCES

Croft, Harry & Parker, Chris. I Always Sit With My Back To The Wall: Managing Traumatic Stress and Combat PTSD. (2011)

Grinder, John & Bandler, Richard. Frogs Into Princes: Neurolinguistic Programming. (1989)

LeDoux, Joseph. The Emotional Brain: The Mysterious Underpinnings of Emotional Life (1998) and The Synaptic Self: How Our Brains Become Who We Are (2003)

Sargent, Allen. The Other Mind's Eye: The Gateway To The Hidden Treasures Of Your Mind. (1999)

ABOUT THE AUTHORS

Jonathan Rice, Ph.D. is a Clinical Psychologist and Master Trainer in Neurolinguistic Programming who has been in private practice since 1981 (California, New Mexico and Texas). Prior to entering private practice, he served as Director of Children's Day Treatment for Merced County Mental Health Services (CA) and Director of Monterrey County Youth and Family Services (CA). In the 70's and 80's, he studied extensively with Victor Frankel, Sidney Jouard, Harold Greenwald, Everet Shostrum, Virginia Satir, Milton Erickson, John Grinder and Leslie Cameron. From 1981 until 1991, he taught advanced therapeutic techniques throughout the United States, Canada and Denmark. From 1991 through 2000, he was a Partner and Clinical Director of the Institute of NLP and Hypnosis in Austin, Tx. In 2003, Dr. Rice devised the first of a series of therapeutic techniques using direct intervention with the client's brain functioning and thinking patterns that are known as BRAIN-SWITCH, now developed into a highly successful system of brain researched techniques for clinical intervention in mood disorders, PTSD, fears/phobias, addiction and other disorders. He received his Ph.D. in Clinical and Counseling Psychology at the United States International University (originated by Carl Rogers, Ph.D., the first "Humanistic Psychology" program in the United States). He currently lives in San Antonio, TX with his wife, Carol, and two cats: Oreo and Sam.

Judi Craig, Ph.D. is a Clinical Psychologist, Executive Coach and Master Practitioner in Neurolinguistic Programming. Her clinical practice involves working with adults, children, teens and couples for over 30 years. She also coaches executives, business owners and professionals on enhancing leadership, improving "people skills", facilitating powerful communication, increasing business/sales and taking charge of their careers. She has been interviewed on over 100 radio stations and appeared on national television (Larry King Live, The Today Show, NBC News, CBS News, Geraldo and more). She has five nationally published books (most recently, WOMEN ATTORNEYS SPEAK OUT!). As a keynote speaker, she has addressed audiences as diverse as the executives of CBS Television to the rescue and service workers of the Oklahoma City bombing, and currently gives presentations both on clinical topics as well as a variety of coaching-related business topics. She received her B.A. from Southern Methodist University and her M.S. and Ph.D. from the University of Wisconsin. She is also a graduate of CoachU and Corporate Coach U and holds the Master Certified Coach credential. She lives with her husband, Jim Norris, a dog named Karma and two cats: Rorschach and Pilgrim.

If you are using the BRAIN-SWITCH process and have either a comment or a question, you are welcome to email us at:

judi@brain-switch.com

jonathan@brain-switch.com

FOR 1-DAY WORKSHOPS ON BRAIN-SWITCH

Please contact

judi@brain-switch.com

or phone (210) 824-3391 or (210) 913-2113

FOR SUPERVISION

Please contact

jonathan@brain-switch.com

or phone (210) 858-2060

NOTES

NOTES

Made in the USA
San Bernardino, CA
11 October 2016